MW00902519

DELICIOUS RECIPES COOKBOOK BY

_____

Canela Journals

Table of contents

Date	Recipe Name	Page

Recipe: _____

Serving: _____   Prep Time: _____

Cook Time: _____   Temperature: _____

Ingredients: Instructions:

_____   _____
_____   _____
_____   _____
_____   _____
_____   _____
_____   _____
_____   _____
_____   _____
_____   _____
_____   _____
_____   _____
_____   _____
_____   _____
_____   _____
_____   _____
_____   _____
_____   _____
_____   _____

Wine Pairing: _____

Notes:

Recipe: _____

Serving: _____   Prep Time: _____

Cook Time: _____   Temperature: _____

Ingredients: Instructions:

_____   _____
_____   _____
_____   _____
_____   _____
_____   _____
_____   _____
_____   _____
_____   _____
_____   _____
_____   _____
_____   _____
_____   _____
_____   _____
_____   _____
_____   _____
_____   _____
_____   _____

Wine Pairing: _____

Notes: _____

Recipe: _____

Serving: _____   Prep Time: _____

Cook Time: _____   Temperature: _____

Ingredients: Instructions:

_____   _____
_____   _____
_____   _____
_____   _____
_____   _____
_____   _____
_____   _____
_____   _____
_____   _____
_____   _____
_____   _____
_____   _____
_____   _____
_____   _____
_____   _____
_____   _____
_____   _____

Wine Pairing: _____

Notes: _____

Recipe: _____

Serving: _____   Prep Time: _____

Cook Time: _____   Temperature: _____

Ingredients:

_____

_____

_____

_____

_____

_____

_____

_____

_____

_____

_____

_____

_____

_____

_____

_____

_____

Instructions:

_____

_____

_____

_____

_____

_____

_____

_____

_____

_____

_____

_____

_____

_____

_____

_____

_____

Wine Pairing: _____

Notes: _____

Recipe: _____

Serving: _____   Prep Time: _____

Cook Time: _____   Temperature: _____

Ingredients: Instructions:

_____   _____
_____   _____
_____   _____
_____   _____
_____   _____
_____   _____
_____   _____
_____   _____
_____   _____
_____   _____
_____   _____
_____   _____
_____   _____
_____   _____
_____   _____
_____   _____
_____   _____
_____   _____
_____   _____

Wine Pairing: _____

Notes: _____

Recipe: _____

Serving: _____   Prep Time: _____

Cook Time: _____   Temperature: _____

Ingredients: Instructions:

_____   _____
_____   _____
_____   _____
_____   _____
_____   _____
_____   _____
_____   _____
_____   _____
_____   _____
_____   _____
_____   _____
_____   _____
_____   _____
_____   _____
_____   _____
_____   _____

Wine Pairing: _____

Notes:

Recipe: _____

Serving: _____   Prep Time: _____

Cook Time: _____   Temperature: _____

Ingredients: Instructions:

_____   _____
_____   _____
_____   _____
_____   _____
_____   _____
_____   _____
_____   _____
_____   _____
_____   _____
_____   _____
_____   _____
_____   _____
_____   _____
_____   _____
_____   _____
_____   _____

Wine Pairing: _____

Notes: _____

Recipe: _____

Serving: _____ Prep Time: _____

Cook Time: _____ Temperature: _____

Ingredients: Instructions:

_____ _____
_____ _____
_____ _____
_____ _____
_____ _____
_____ _____
_____ _____
_____ _____
_____ _____
_____ _____
_____ _____
_____ _____
_____ _____
_____ _____
_____ _____
_____ _____

Wine Pairing: _____

Notes: _____

Recipe: _____

Serving: _____   Prep Time: _____

Cook Time: _____   Temperature: _____

Ingredients: Instructions:

_____   _____
_____   _____
_____   _____
_____   _____
_____   _____
_____   _____
_____   _____
_____   _____
_____   _____
_____   _____
_____   _____
_____   _____
_____   _____
_____   _____
_____   _____
_____   _____
_____   _____

Wine Pairing: _____

Notes: _____

Recipe: _____

Serving: _____   Prep Time: _____

Cook Time: _____   Temperature: _____

Ingredients: Instructions:

_____   _____
_____   _____
_____   _____
_____   _____
_____   _____
_____   _____
_____   _____
_____   _____
_____   _____
_____   _____
_____   _____
_____   _____
_____   _____
_____   _____
_____   _____
_____   _____

Wine Pairing: _____

Notes: _____

Recipe: _____

Serving: _____   Prep Time: _____

Cook Time: _____   Temperature: _____

Ingredients: Instructions:

_____   _____
_____   _____
_____   _____
_____   _____
_____   _____
_____   _____
_____   _____
_____   _____
_____   _____
_____   _____
_____   _____
_____   _____
_____   _____
_____   _____
_____   _____
_____   _____
_____   _____

Wine Pairing: _____

Notes: _____

Recipe:

Serving: Prep Time:

Cook Time: Temperature:

Ingredients: Instructions:

Wine Pairing:

Notes:

Recipe: _____

Serving: _____   Prep Time: _____

Cook Time: _____   Temperature: _____

Ingredients: Instructions:

_____   _____
_____   _____
_____   _____
_____   _____
_____   _____
_____   _____
_____   _____
_____   _____
_____   _____
_____   _____
_____   _____
_____   _____
_____   _____
_____   _____
_____   _____
_____   _____
_____   _____

Wine Pairing: _____

Notes: _____

Recipe:

Serving: _____ Prep Time: _____

Cook Time: _____ Temperature: _____

Ingredients: Instructions:

Wine Pairing: _____

Notes:

Recipe:

Serving: _____   Prep Time: _____

Cook Time: _____   Temperature: _____

Ingredients: Instructions:

Wine Pairing: _____

Notes:

Recipe: _____

Serving: _____ Prep Time: _____

Cook Time: _____ Temperature: _____

Ingredients:

_____

_____

_____

_____

_____

_____

_____

_____

_____

_____

_____

_____

_____

_____

Instructions:

_____

_____

_____

_____

_____

_____

_____

_____

_____

_____

_____

_____

_____

_____

Wine Pairing: _____

Notes:

Recipe: _____

Serving: _____   Prep Time: _____

Cook Time: _____   Temperature: _____

Ingredients: Instructions:

_____   _____
_____   _____
_____   _____
_____   _____
_____   _____
_____   _____
_____   _____
_____   _____
_____   _____
_____   _____
_____   _____
_____   _____
_____   _____
_____   _____
_____   _____
_____   _____
_____   _____
_____   _____

Wine Pairing: _____

Notes:

Recipe:

Serving: _____   Prep Time: _____

Cook Time: _____   Temperature: _____

Ingredients: Instructions:

_____   _____
_____   _____
_____   _____
_____   _____
_____   _____
_____   _____
_____   _____
_____   _____
_____   _____
_____   _____
_____   _____
_____   _____
_____   _____
_____   _____
_____   _____
_____   _____

Wine Pairing: _____

Notes: _____

Recipe: _____

Serving: _____ Prep Time: _____

Cook Time: _____ Temperature: _____

Ingredients: Instructions:

Wine Pairing: _____

Notes:

Recipe:

Serving: _____   Prep Time: _____

Cook Time: _____   Temperature: _____

Ingredients: Instructions:

Wine Pairing: _____

Notes:

Recipe: _____

Serving: _____ Prep Time: _____

Cook Time: _____ Temperature: _____

Ingredients: Instructions:

_____ _____
_____ _____
_____ _____
_____ _____
_____ _____
_____ _____
_____ _____
_____ _____
_____ _____
_____ _____
_____ _____
_____ _____
_____ _____
_____ _____
_____ _____
_____ _____

Wine Pairing: _____

Notes: _____

Recipe: _____

Serving: _____   Prep Time: _____

Cook Time: _____   Temperature: _____

Ingredients: Instructions:

_____   _____
_____   _____
_____   _____
_____   _____
_____   _____
_____   _____
_____   _____
_____   _____
_____   _____
_____   _____
_____   _____
_____   _____
_____   _____
_____   _____
_____   _____
_____   _____

Wine Pairing: _____

Notes: _____

Recipe: _____

Serving: _____   Prep Time: _____

Cook Time: _____   Temperature: _____

Ingredients: Instructions:

_____   _____
_____   _____
_____   _____
_____   _____
_____   _____
_____   _____
_____   _____
_____   _____
_____   _____
_____   _____
_____   _____
_____   _____
_____   _____
_____   _____
_____   _____
_____   _____
_____   _____

Wine Pairing: _____

Notes: _____

Recipe:

Serving: _____ Prep Time: _____

Cook Time: _____ Temperature: _____

Ingredients: Instructions:

Wine Pairing: _____

Notes:

Recipe:

Serving: _____   Prep Time: _____

Cook Time: _____   Temperature: _____

Ingredients: Instructions:

Wine Pairing: _____

Notes:

Recipe: _____

Serving: _____   Prep Time: _____

Cook Time: _____   Temperature: _____

Ingredients: Instructions:

_____   _____
_____   _____
_____   _____
_____   _____
_____   _____
_____   _____
_____   _____
_____   _____
_____   _____
_____   _____
_____   _____
_____   _____
_____   _____
_____   _____
_____   _____
_____   _____

Wine Pairing: _____

Notes: _____

Recipe: _____

Serving: _____   Prep Time: _____

Cook Time: _____   Temperature: _____

Ingredients: Instructions:

_____   _____
_____   _____
_____   _____
_____   _____
_____   _____
_____   _____
_____   _____
_____   _____
_____   _____
_____   _____
_____   _____
_____   _____
_____   _____
_____   _____
_____   _____
_____   _____
_____   _____

Wine Pairing: _____

Notes:

Recipe:

Serving: _____   Prep Time: _____

Cook Time: _____   Temperature: _____

Ingredients: Instructions:

_____   _____
_____   _____
_____   _____
_____   _____
_____   _____
_____   _____
_____   _____
_____   _____
_____   _____
_____   _____
_____   _____
_____   _____
_____   _____
_____   _____
_____   _____
_____   _____

Wine Pairing: _____

Notes: _____

Recipe:

Serving: Prep Time:

Cook Time: Temperature:

Ingredients: Instructions:

Wine Pairing:

Notes:

Recipe: _____

Serving: _____   Prep Time: _____

Cook Time: _____   Temperature: _____

Ingredients: Instructions:

_____   _____
_____   _____
_____   _____
_____   _____
_____   _____
_____   _____
_____   _____
_____   _____
_____   _____
_____   _____
_____   _____
_____   _____
_____   _____
_____   _____
_____   _____
_____   _____
_____   _____

Wine Pairing: _____

Notes: _____

Recipe:

Serving: _____   Prep Time: _____

Cook Time: _____   Temperature: _____

Ingredients: Instructions:

Wine Pairing: _____

Notes:

Recipe: _____

Serving: _____   Prep Time: _____

Cook Time: _____   Temperature: _____

Ingredients: Instructions:

_____   _____
_____   _____
_____   _____
_____   _____
_____   _____
_____   _____
_____   _____
_____   _____
_____   _____
_____   _____
_____   _____
_____   _____
_____   _____
_____   _____
_____   _____
_____   _____

Wine Pairing: _____

Notes: _____

Recipe: _____

Serving: _____   Prep Time: _____

Cook Time: _____   Temperature: _____

Ingredients: Instructions:

_____   _____
_____   _____
_____   _____
_____   _____
_____   _____
_____   _____
_____   _____
_____   _____
_____   _____
_____   _____
_____   _____
_____   _____
_____   _____
_____   _____
_____   _____
_____   _____
_____   _____

Wine Pairing: _____

Notes: _____

Recipe:

Serving: Prep Time:

Cook Time: Temperature:

Ingredients: Instructions:

Wine Pairing:

Notes:

Recipe:

Serving: Prep Time:

Cook Time: Temperature:

Ingredients: Instructions:

Wine Pairing:

Notes:

Recipe: _____

Serving: _____   Prep Time: _____

Cook Time: _____   Temperature: _____

Ingredients: Instructions:

_____   _____
_____   _____
_____   _____
_____   _____
_____   _____
_____   _____
_____   _____
_____   _____
_____   _____
_____   _____
_____   _____
_____   _____
_____   _____
_____   _____
_____   _____
_____   _____

Wine Pairing: _____

Notes: _____

Recipe: _____

Serving: _____ Prep Time: _____

Cook Time: _____ Temperature: _____

Ingredients: Instructions:

_____ _____
_____ _____
_____ _____
_____ _____
_____ _____
_____ _____
_____ _____
_____ _____
_____ _____
_____ _____
_____ _____
_____ _____
_____ _____
_____ _____
_____ _____
_____ _____

Wine Pairing: _____

Notes: _____

Recipe: _____

Serving: _____   Prep Time: _____

Cook Time: _____   Temperature: _____

Ingredients: Instructions:

Wine Pairing: _____

Notes: _____

Recipe:

Serving: _____ Prep Time: _____

Cook Time: _____ Temperature: _____

Ingredients: | Instructions:

Wine Pairing: _____

Notes:

Recipe:

Serving: _____   Prep Time: _____

Cook Time: _____   Temperature: _____

Ingredients: Instructions:

Wine Pairing: _____

Notes:

Recipe: _____

Serving: _____   Prep Time: _____

Cook Time: _____   Temperature: _____

Ingredients: | Instructions:

_____   _____

_____   _____

_____   _____

_____   _____

_____   _____

_____   _____

_____   _____

_____   _____

_____   _____

_____   _____

_____   _____

_____   _____

_____   _____

_____   _____

_____   _____

_____   _____

_____   _____

Wine Pairing: _____

Notes: _____

Recipe: _____

Serving: _____   Prep Time: _____

Cook Time: _____   Temperature: _____

Ingredients: Instructions:

_____   _____
_____   _____
_____   _____
_____   _____
_____   _____
_____   _____
_____   _____
_____   _____
_____   _____
_____   _____
_____   _____
_____   _____
_____   _____
_____   _____
_____   _____

Wine Pairing: _____

Notes: _____

Recipe: _____

Serving: _____   Prep Time: _____

Cook Time: _____   Temperature: _____

Ingredients: Instructions:

_____   _____
_____   _____
_____   _____
_____   _____
_____   _____
_____   _____
_____   _____
_____   _____
_____   _____
_____   _____
_____   _____
_____   _____
_____   _____
_____   _____
_____   _____

Wine Pairing: _____

Notes: _____

Recipe:

Serving: _____   Prep Time: _____

Cook Time: _____   Temperature: _____

Ingredients: Instructions:

_____   _____
_____   _____
_____   _____
_____   _____
_____   _____
_____   _____
_____   _____
_____   _____
_____   _____
_____   _____
_____   _____
_____   _____
_____   _____
_____   _____
_____   _____
_____   _____

Wine Pairing: _____

Notes: _____

Recipe: _____

Serving: _____   Prep Time: _____

Cook Time: _____   Temperature: _____

Ingredients: Instructions:

_____   _____
_____   _____
_____   _____
_____   _____
_____   _____
_____   _____
_____   _____
_____   _____
_____   _____
_____   _____
_____   _____
_____   _____
_____   _____
_____   _____
_____   _____
_____   _____

Wine Pairing: _____

Notes: _____

Recipe:

Serving: _____   Prep Time: _____

Cook Time: _____   Temperature: _____

Ingredients: Instructions:

_____   _____
_____   _____
_____   _____
_____   _____
_____   _____
_____   _____
_____   _____
_____   _____
_____   _____
_____   _____
_____   _____
_____   _____
_____   _____
_____   _____
_____   _____

Wine Pairing: _____

Notes:

Recipe:

Serving: _____ Prep Time: _____

Cook Time: _____ Temperature: _____

Ingredients: Instructions:

Wine Pairing: _____

Notes: _____

Recipe: _____

Serving: _____   Prep Time: _____

Cook Time: _____   Temperature: _____

Ingredients: Instructions:

_____   _____
_____   _____
_____   _____
_____   _____
_____   _____
_____   _____
_____   _____
_____   _____
_____   _____
_____   _____
_____   _____
_____   _____
_____   _____
_____   _____
_____   _____
_____   _____
_____   _____

Wine Pairing: _____

Notes: _____

Recipe:

Serving: Prep Time:

Cook Time: Temperature:

Ingredients: Instructions:

_____   _____
_____   _____
_____   _____
_____   _____
_____   _____
_____   _____
_____   _____
_____   _____
_____   _____
_____   _____
_____   _____
_____   _____
_____   _____
_____   _____
_____   _____
_____   _____
_____   _____

Wine Pairing:

Notes:

Recipe: _____

Serving: _____   Prep Time: _____

Cook Time: _____   Temperature: _____

Ingredients: Instructions:

_____   _____
_____   _____
_____   _____
_____   _____
_____   _____
_____   _____
_____   _____
_____   _____
_____   _____
_____   _____
_____   _____
_____   _____
_____   _____
_____   _____
_____   _____
_____   _____

Wine Pairing: _____

Notes: _____

Recipe: _____

Serving: _____   Prep Time: _____

Cook Time: _____   Temperature: _____

Ingredients: Instructions:

_____   _____
_____   _____
_____   _____
_____   _____
_____   _____
_____   _____
_____   _____
_____   _____
_____   _____
_____   _____
_____   _____
_____   _____
_____   _____
_____   _____
_____   _____
_____   _____

Wine Pairing: _____

Notes: _____

Recipe:

Serving: _____   Prep Time: _____

Cook Time: _____   Temperature: _____

Ingredients: Instructions:

Wine Pairing: _____

Notes: _____

Recipe: _____

Serving: _____   Prep Time: _____

Cook Time: _____   Temperature: _____

Ingredients: Instructions:

_____   _____
_____   _____
_____   _____
_____   _____
_____   _____
_____   _____
_____   _____
_____   _____
_____   _____
_____   _____
_____   _____
_____   _____
_____   _____
_____   _____
_____   _____
_____   _____

Wine Pairing: _____

Notes: _____

Recipe: _____

Serving: _____   Prep Time: _____

Cook Time: _____   Temperature: _____

Ingredients: Instructions:

_____   _____
_____   _____
_____   _____
_____   _____
_____   _____
_____   _____
_____   _____
_____   _____
_____   _____
_____   _____
_____   _____
_____   _____
_____   _____
_____   _____
_____   _____

Wine Pairing: _____

Notes: _____

Recipe:

Serving: _____   Prep Time: _____

Cook Time: _____   Temperature: _____

Ingredients: Instructions:

Wine Pairing: _____

Notes:

Recipe: _____

Serving: _____   Prep Time: _____

Cook Time: _____   Temperature: _____

Ingredients: Instructions:

_____   _____
_____   _____
_____   _____
_____   _____
_____   _____
_____   _____
_____   _____
_____   _____
_____   _____
_____   _____
_____   _____
_____   _____
_____   _____
_____   _____
_____   _____
_____   _____

Wine Pairing: _____

Notes: _____

Recipe:

Serving: _____ Prep Time: _____

Cook Time: _____ Temperature: _____

Ingredients: Instructions:

Wine Pairing: _____

Notes: _____

Recipe: _____

Serving: _____   Prep Time: _____

Cook Time: _____   Temperature: _____

Ingredients: Instructions:

_____   _____
_____   _____
_____   _____
_____   _____
_____   _____
_____   _____
_____   _____
_____   _____
_____   _____
_____   _____
_____   _____
_____   _____
_____   _____
_____   _____
_____   _____
_____   _____

Wine Pairing: _____

Notes: _____

Recipe: _____

Serving: _____   Prep Time: _____

Cook Time: _____   Temperature: _____

Ingredients: Instructions:

_____   _____
_____   _____
_____   _____
_____   _____
_____   _____
_____   _____
_____   _____
_____   _____
_____   _____
_____   _____
_____   _____
_____   _____
_____   _____
_____   _____
_____   _____
_____   _____
_____   _____

Wine Pairing: _____

Notes: _____

Recipe: _____

Serving: _____   Prep Time: _____

Cook Time: _____   Temperature: _____

Ingredients: Instructions:

_____   _____
_____   _____
_____   _____
_____   _____
_____   _____
_____   _____
_____   _____
_____   _____
_____   _____
_____   _____
_____   _____
_____   _____
_____   _____
_____   _____

Wine Pairing: _____

Notes: _____

Recipe:

Serving: _____ Prep Time: _____

Cook Time: _____ Temperature: _____

Ingredients:

Instructions:

Wine Pairing: _____

Notes:

Recipe: _____

Serving: _____   Prep Time: _____

Cook Time: _____   Temperature: _____

Ingredients: Instructions:

_____   _____
_____   _____
_____   _____
_____   _____
_____   _____
_____   _____
_____   _____
_____   _____
_____   _____
_____   _____
_____   _____
_____   _____
_____   _____
_____   _____
_____   _____

Wine Pairing: _____

Notes: _____

Recipe: _____

Serving: _____   Prep Time: _____

Cook Time: _____   Temperature: _____

Ingredients: Instructions:

_____   _____
_____   _____
_____   _____
_____   _____
_____   _____
_____   _____
_____   _____
_____   _____
_____   _____
_____   _____
_____   _____
_____   _____
_____   _____
_____   _____
_____   _____
_____   _____
_____   _____

Wine Pairing: _____

Notes: _____

Recipe:

Serving: _____   Prep Time: _____

Cook Time: _____   Temperature: _____

Ingredients: Instructions:

Wine Pairing: _____

Notes:

Recipe: _____

Serving: _____   Prep Time: _____

Cook Time: _____   Temperature: _____

Ingredients: Instructions:

_____   _____
_____   _____
_____   _____
_____   _____
_____   _____
_____   _____
_____   _____
_____   _____
_____   _____
_____   _____
_____   _____
_____   _____
_____   _____
_____   _____
_____   _____

Wine Pairing: _____

Notes: _____

Recipe:

Serving: _____   Prep Time: _____

Cook Time: _____   Temperature: _____

Ingredients: Instructions:

_____   _____
_____   _____
_____   _____
_____   _____
_____   _____
_____   _____
_____   _____
_____   _____
_____   _____
_____   _____
_____   _____
_____   _____
_____   _____
_____   _____
_____   _____
_____   _____

Wine Pairing: _____

Notes: _____

Recipe: _____

Serving: _____   Prep Time: _____

Cook Time: _____   Temperature: _____

Ingredients: Instructions:

_____   _____
_____   _____
_____   _____
_____   _____
_____   _____
_____   _____
_____   _____
_____   _____
_____   _____
_____   _____
_____   _____
_____   _____
_____   _____
_____   _____
_____   _____
_____   _____

Wine Pairing: _____

Notes: _____

Recipe:

Serving: _____ Prep Time: _____

Cook Time: _____ Temperature: _____

Ingredients: Instructions:

Wine Pairing: _____

Notes:

Recipe: _____

Serving: _____   Prep Time: _____

Cook Time: _____   Temperature: _____

Ingredients: Instructions:

_____   _____
_____   _____
_____   _____
_____   _____
_____   _____
_____   _____
_____   _____
_____   _____
_____   _____
_____   _____
_____   _____
_____   _____
_____   _____
_____   _____
_____   _____
_____   _____

Wine Pairing: _____

Notes: _____

Recipe: _____

Serving: _____   Prep Time: _____

Cook Time: _____   Temperature: _____

Ingredients: Instructions:

_____   _____
_____   _____
_____   _____
_____   _____
_____   _____
_____   _____
_____   _____
_____   _____
_____   _____
_____   _____
_____   _____
_____   _____
_____   _____
_____   _____
_____   _____

Wine Pairing: _____

Notes: _____

Recipe:

Serving: _____   Prep Time: _____

Cook Time: _____   Temperature: _____

Ingredients: Instructions:

_____   _____
_____   _____
_____   _____
_____   _____
_____   _____
_____   _____
_____   _____
_____   _____
_____   _____
_____   _____
_____   _____
_____   _____
_____   _____
_____   _____
_____   _____
_____   _____

Wine Pairing: _____

Notes: _____

Recipe:

Serving: _____ Prep Time: _____

Cook Time: _____ Temperature: _____

Ingredients: Instructions:

Wine Pairing: _____

Notes:

Recipe: _____

Serving: _____   Prep Time: _____

Cook Time: _____   Temperature: _____

Ingredients: Instructions:

_____   _____
_____   _____
_____   _____
_____   _____
_____   _____
_____   _____
_____   _____
_____   _____
_____   _____
_____   _____
_____   _____
_____   _____
_____   _____
_____   _____
_____   _____
_____   _____
_____   _____

Wine Pairing: _____

Notes: _____

Recipe:

Serving: _____ Prep Time: _____

Cook Time: _____ Temperature: _____

Ingredients: Instructions:

Wine Pairing: _____

Notes:

Recipe:

Serving: _____ Prep Time: _____

Cook Time: _____ Temperature: _____

Ingredients: Instructions:

Wine Pairing: _____

Notes:

Recipe:

Serving: _____ Prep Time: _____

Cook Time: _____ Temperature: _____

Ingredients: Instructions:

Wine Pairing: _____

Notes:

Recipe:

Serving: _____ Prep Time: _____

Cook Time: _____ Temperature: _____

Ingredients: Instructions:

Wine Pairing: _____

Notes:

Recipe: _____

Serving: _____   Prep Time: _____

Cook Time: _____   Temperature: _____

Ingredients: Instructions:

_____   _____
_____   _____
_____   _____
_____   _____
_____   _____
_____   _____
_____   _____
_____   _____
_____   _____
_____   _____
_____   _____
_____   _____
_____   _____
_____   _____
_____   _____
_____   _____
_____   _____

Wine Pairing: _____

Notes: _____

Recipe: _____

Serving: _____   Prep Time: _____

Cook Time: _____   Temperature: _____

Ingredients: Instructions:

_____   _____
_____   _____
_____   _____
_____   _____
_____   _____
_____   _____
_____   _____
_____   _____
_____   _____
_____   _____
_____   _____
_____   _____
_____   _____
_____   _____
_____   _____
_____   _____

Wine Pairing: _____

Notes: _____

Recipe:

Serving: _____   Prep Time: _____

Cook Time: _____   Temperature: _____

Ingredients: Instructions:

Wine Pairing: _____

Notes:

Recipe: _____

Serving: _____   Prep Time: _____

Cook Time: _____   Temperature: _____

Ingredients: Instructions:

_____   _____
_____   _____
_____   _____
_____   _____
_____   _____
_____   _____
_____   _____
_____   _____
_____   _____
_____   _____
_____   _____
_____   _____
_____   _____
_____   _____
_____   _____
_____   _____

Wine Pairing: _____

Notes: _____

Recipe:

Serving: _____ Prep Time: _____

Cook Time: _____ Temperature: _____

Ingredients: Instructions:

Wine Pairing: _____

Notes:

Recipe:

Serving: _____ Prep Time: _____

Cook Time: _____ Temperature: _____

Ingredients: Instructions:

_____ _____
_____ _____
_____ _____
_____ _____
_____ _____
_____ _____
_____ _____
_____ _____
_____ _____
_____ _____
_____ _____
_____ _____
_____ _____
_____ _____
_____ _____
_____ _____

Wine Pairing: _____

Notes: _____

Recipe: _____

Serving: _____   Prep Time: _____

Cook Time: _____   Temperature: _____

Ingredients: Instructions:

_____   _____
_____   _____
_____   _____
_____   _____
_____   _____
_____   _____
_____   _____
_____   _____
_____   _____
_____   _____
_____   _____
_____   _____
_____   _____
_____   _____
_____   _____
_____   _____
_____   _____

Wine Pairing: _____

Notes: _____

Recipe: _____

Serving: _____   Prep Time: _____

Cook Time: _____   Temperature: _____

Ingredients: Instructions:

_____   _____
_____   _____
_____   _____
_____   _____
_____   _____
_____   _____
_____   _____
_____   _____
_____   _____
_____   _____
_____   _____
_____   _____
_____   _____
_____   _____
_____   _____
_____   _____

Wine Pairing: _____

Notes: _____

Recipe: _____

Serving: _____   Prep Time: _____

Cook Time: _____   Temperature: _____

Ingredients: Instructions:

_____   _____
_____   _____
_____   _____
_____   _____
_____   _____
_____   _____
_____   _____
_____   _____
_____   _____
_____   _____
_____   _____
_____   _____
_____   _____
_____   _____
_____   _____

Wine Pairing: _____

Notes: _____

Recipe: _____

Serving: _____   Prep Time: _____

Cook Time: _____   Temperature: _____

Ingredients: Instructions:

_____   _____
_____   _____
_____   _____
_____   _____
_____   _____
_____   _____
_____   _____
_____   _____
_____   _____
_____   _____
_____   _____
_____   _____
_____   _____
_____   _____
_____   _____
_____   _____
_____   _____

Wine Pairing: _____

Notes: _____

Recipe: _____

Serving: _____ Prep Time: _____

Cook Time: _____ Temperature: _____

Ingredients: Instructions:

_____ _____
_____ _____
_____ _____
_____ _____
_____ _____
_____ _____
_____ _____
_____ _____
_____ _____
_____ _____
_____ _____
_____ _____
_____ _____
_____ _____
_____ _____
_____ _____

Wine Pairing: _____

Notes: _____

Recipe:

Serving: _____ Prep Time: _____

Cook Time: _____ Temperature: _____

Ingredients: Instructions:

Wine Pairing: _____

Notes: _____

Recipe: _____

Serving: _____   Prep Time: _____

Cook Time: _____   Temperature: _____

Ingredients: Instructions:

_____   _____
_____   _____
_____   _____
_____   _____
_____   _____
_____   _____
_____   _____
_____   _____
_____   _____
_____   _____
_____   _____
_____   _____
_____   _____
_____   _____
_____   _____
_____   _____
_____   _____
_____   _____

Wine Pairing: _____

Notes: _____

Recipe:

Serving: Prep Time:

Cook Time: Temperature:

Ingredients: Instructions:

Wine Pairing:

Notes:

Recipe:

Serving: _____ Prep Time: _____

Cook Time: _____ Temperature: _____

Ingredients: Instructions:

_____   _____
_____   _____
_____   _____
_____   _____
_____   _____
_____   _____
_____   _____
_____   _____
_____   _____
_____   _____
_____   _____
_____   _____
_____   _____
_____   _____
_____   _____
_____   _____

Wine Pairing: _____

Notes: _____

Recipe: _____

Serving: _____ Prep Time: _____

Cook Time: _____ Temperature: _____

Ingredients: Instructions:

_____ _____
_____ _____
_____ _____
_____ _____
_____ _____
_____ _____
_____ _____
_____ _____
_____ _____
_____ _____
_____ _____
_____ _____
_____ _____
_____ _____
_____ _____
_____ _____
_____ _____
_____ _____

Wine Pairing: _____

Notes: _____

Recipe:

Serving: _____   Prep Time: _____

Cook Time: _____   Temperature: _____

Ingredients: Instructions:

_____   _____
_____   _____
_____   _____
_____   _____
_____   _____
_____   _____
_____   _____
_____   _____
_____   _____
_____   _____
_____   _____
_____   _____
_____   _____
_____   _____
_____   _____

Wine Pairing: _____

Notes: _____

Recipe:

Serving: _____   Prep Time: _____

Cook Time: _____   Temperature: _____

Ingredients: Instructions:

_____   _____
_____   _____
_____   _____
_____   _____
_____   _____
_____   _____
_____   _____
_____   _____
_____   _____
_____   _____
_____   _____
_____   _____
_____   _____
_____   _____
_____   _____
_____   _____
_____   _____

Wine Pairing: _____

Notes: _____

Recipe:

Serving: _____ Prep Time: _____

Cook Time: _____ Temperature: _____

Ingredients: Instructions:

Wine Pairing: _____

Notes:

Recipe:

Serving: _____   Prep Time: _____

Cook Time: _____   Temperature: _____

Ingredients: Instructions:

Wine Pairing: _____

Notes:

Recipe:

Serving: _____ Prep Time: _____

Cook Time: _____ Temperature: _____

Ingredients: Instructions:

Wine Pairing: _____

Notes:

Recipe:

Serving: _____ **Prep Time:** _____

Cook Time: _____ **Temperature:** _____

Ingredients: **Instructions:**

_____   _____
_____   _____
_____   _____
_____   _____
_____   _____
_____   _____
_____   _____
_____   _____
_____   _____
_____   _____
_____   _____
_____   _____
_____   _____
_____   _____
_____   _____
_____   _____

Wine Pairing: _____

Notes: _____

Recipe: _____

Serving: _____ Prep Time: _____

Cook Time: _____ Temperature: _____

Ingredients: Instructions:

_____ _____
_____ _____
_____ _____
_____ _____
_____ _____
_____ _____
_____ _____
_____ _____
_____ _____
_____ _____
_____ _____
_____ _____
_____ _____
_____ _____
_____ _____
_____ _____

Wine Pairing: _____

Notes: _____

Recipe:

Serving: _____ Prep Time: _____

Cook Time: _____ Temperature: _____

Ingredients:

Instructions:

Wine Pairing: _____

Notes: _____

Recipe: _____

Serving: _____   Prep Time: _____

Cook Time: _____   Temperature: _____

Ingredients: Instructions:

_____   _____
_____   _____
_____   _____
_____   _____
_____   _____
_____   _____
_____   _____
_____   _____
_____   _____
_____   _____
_____   _____
_____   _____
_____   _____
_____   _____
_____   _____

Wine Pairing: _____

Notes: _____

Recipe: _____

Serving: _____   Prep Time: _____

Cook Time: _____   Temperature: _____

Ingredients: Instructions:

_____   _____
_____   _____
_____   _____
_____   _____
_____   _____
_____   _____
_____   _____
_____   _____
_____   _____
_____   _____
_____   _____
_____   _____
_____   _____
_____   _____
_____   _____
_____   _____
_____   _____

Wine Pairing: _____

Notes: _____

Recipe: _____

Serving: _____   Prep Time: _____

Cook Time: _____   Temperature: _____

Ingredients: Instructions:

_____   _____
_____   _____
_____   _____
_____   _____
_____   _____
_____   _____
_____   _____
_____   _____
_____   _____
_____   _____
_____   _____
_____   _____
_____   _____
_____   _____
_____   _____
_____   _____

Wine Pairing: _____

Notes: _____

Recipe: _____

Serving: _____   Prep Time: _____

Cook Time: _____   Temperature: _____

Ingredients: Instructions:

_____   _____
_____   _____
_____   _____
_____   _____
_____   _____
_____   _____
_____   _____
_____   _____
_____   _____
_____   _____
_____   _____
_____   _____
_____   _____
_____   _____
_____   _____
_____   _____

Wine Pairing: _____

Notes: _____

Recipe: _____

Serving: _____   Prep Time: _____

Cook Time: _____   Temperature: _____

Ingredients: Instructions:

_____   _____
_____   _____
_____   _____
_____   _____
_____   _____
_____   _____
_____   _____
_____   _____
_____   _____
_____   _____
_____   _____
_____   _____
_____   _____
_____   _____
_____   _____
_____   _____

Wine Pairing: _____

Notes: _____

Recipe: _____

Serving: _____ Prep Time: _____

Cook Time: _____ Temperature: _____

Ingredients: Instructions:

_____ _____
_____ _____
_____ _____
_____ _____
_____ _____
_____ _____
_____ _____
_____ _____
_____ _____
_____ _____
_____ _____
_____ _____
_____ _____
_____ _____
_____ _____
_____ _____

Wine Pairing: _____

Notes: _____

Recipe:

Serving: _____   Prep Time: _____

Cook Time: _____   Temperature: _____

Ingredients: Instructions:

_____   _____
_____   _____
_____   _____
_____   _____
_____   _____
_____   _____
_____   _____
_____   _____
_____   _____
_____   _____
_____   _____
_____   _____
_____   _____
_____   _____
_____   _____

Wine Pairing: _____

Notes: _____

Recipe: _____

Serving: _____   Prep Time: _____

Cook Time: _____   Temperature: _____

Ingredients: Instructions:

_____   _____
_____   _____
_____   _____
_____   _____
_____   _____
_____   _____
_____   _____
_____   _____
_____   _____
_____   _____
_____   _____
_____   _____
_____   _____
_____   _____
_____   _____
_____   _____
_____   _____

Wine Pairing: _____

Notes: _____

Recipe:

Serving: _____ Prep Time: _____

Cook Time: _____ Temperature: _____

Ingredients: Instructions:

Wine Pairing: _____

Notes:

Recipe:

Serving: _____   Prep Time: _____

Cook Time: _____   Temperature: _____

Ingredients: Instructions:

Recipe: _____

Serving: _____ Prep Time: _____

Cook Time: _____ Temperature: _____

Ingredients: Instructions:

_____ _____
_____ _____
_____ _____
_____ _____
_____ _____
_____ _____
_____ _____
_____ _____
_____ _____
_____ _____
_____ _____
_____ _____
_____ _____
_____ _____
_____ _____
_____ _____

Wine Pairing: _____

Notes: _____

Recipe:

Serving: _____   Prep Time: _____

Cook Time: _____   Temperature: _____

Ingredients: Instructions:

Wine Pairing: _____

Notes:

Recipe: _____

Serving: _____   Prep Time: _____

Cook Time: _____   Temperature: _____

Ingredients: Instructions:

_____   _____
_____   _____
_____   _____
_____   _____
_____   _____
_____   _____
_____   _____
_____   _____
_____   _____
_____   _____
_____   _____
_____   _____
_____   _____
_____   _____
_____   _____
_____   _____

Wine Pairing: _____

Notes: _____

Recipe:

Serving: _____   Prep Time: _____

Cook Time: _____   Temperature: _____

Ingredients: Instructions:

Wine Pairing: _____

Notes:

Recipe: _____

Serving: _____   Prep Time: _____

Cook Time: _____   Temperature: _____

Ingredients: Instructions:

_____   _____
_____   _____
_____   _____
_____   _____
_____   _____
_____   _____
_____   _____
_____   _____
_____   _____
_____   _____
_____   _____
_____   _____
_____   _____
_____   _____
_____   _____
_____   _____

Wine Pairing: _____

Notes: _____

Recipe:

Serving: _____   Prep Time: _____

Cook Time: _____   Temperature: _____

Ingredients: Instructions:

_____   _____
_____   _____
_____   _____
_____   _____
_____   _____
_____   _____
_____   _____
_____   _____
_____   _____
_____   _____
_____   _____
_____   _____
_____   _____
_____   _____
_____   _____
_____   _____

Wine Pairing: _____

Notes: _____

Recipe: _____

Serving: _____   Prep Time: _____

Cook Time: _____   Temperature: _____

Ingredients: Instructions:

_____   _____
_____   _____
_____   _____
_____   _____
_____   _____
_____   _____
_____   _____
_____   _____
_____   _____
_____   _____
_____   _____
_____   _____
_____   _____
_____   _____
_____   _____

Wine Pairing: _____

Notes: _____

Recipe:

Serving: _____   Prep Time: _____

Cook Time: _____   Temperature: _____

Ingredients: Instructions:

_____   _____
_____   _____
_____   _____
_____   _____
_____   _____
_____   _____
_____   _____
_____   _____
_____   _____
_____   _____
_____   _____
_____   _____
_____   _____
_____   _____
_____   _____
_____   _____

Wine Pairing: _____

Notes: _____

Recipe:

Serving: _____   Prep Time: _____

Cook Time: _____   Temperature: _____

Ingredients: Instructions:

Wine Pairing: _____

Notes:

Recipe: _____

Serving: _____   Prep Time: _____

Cook Time: _____   Temperature: _____

Ingredients: Instructions:

_____   _____
_____   _____
_____   _____
_____   _____
_____   _____
_____   _____
_____   _____
_____   _____
_____   _____
_____   _____
_____   _____
_____   _____
_____   _____
_____   _____
_____   _____
_____   _____

Wine Pairing: _____

Notes:
_____

Recipe:

Serving: _____ Prep Time: _____

Cook Time: _____ Temperature: _____

Ingredients: Instructions:

Wine Pairing: _____

Notes:

Recipe: _____

Serving: _____   Prep Time: _____

Cook Time: _____   Temperature: _____

Ingredients: Instructions:

_____   _____
_____   _____
_____   _____
_____   _____
_____   _____
_____   _____
_____   _____
_____   _____
_____   _____
_____   _____
_____   _____
_____   _____
_____   _____
_____   _____
_____   _____
_____   _____
_____   _____

Wine Pairing: _____

Notes: _____

Recipe: _____

Serving: _____   Prep Time: _____

Cook Time: _____   Temperature: _____

Ingredients: | Instructions:

_____   _____
_____   _____
_____   _____
_____   _____
_____   _____
_____   _____
_____   _____
_____   _____
_____   _____
_____   _____
_____   _____
_____   _____
_____   _____
_____   _____
_____   _____
_____   _____

Wine Pairing: _____

Notes: _____

Recipe: _____

Serving: _____   Prep Time: _____

Cook Time: _____   Temperature: _____

Ingredients: Instructions:

_____   _____
_____   _____
_____   _____
_____   _____
_____   _____
_____   _____
_____   _____
_____   _____
_____   _____
_____   _____
_____   _____
_____   _____
_____   _____
_____   _____
_____   _____

Wine Pairing: _____

Notes: _____

Recipe: _____

Serving: _____ Prep Time: _____

Cook Time: _____ Temperature: _____

Ingredients: Instructions:

_____ _____

_____ _____

_____ _____

_____ _____

_____ _____

_____ _____

_____ _____

_____ _____

_____ _____

_____ _____

_____ _____

_____ _____

_____ _____

_____ _____

_____ _____

Wine Pairing: _____

Notes: _____

Recipe: _____

Serving: _____   Prep Time: _____

Cook Time: _____   Temperature: _____

Ingredients: Instructions:

_____   _____
_____   _____
_____   _____
_____   _____
_____   _____
_____   _____
_____   _____
_____   _____
_____   _____
_____   _____
_____   _____
_____   _____
_____   _____
_____   _____

Wine Pairing: _____

Notes: _____

Recipe:

Serving: _____ Prep Time: _____

Cook Time: _____ Temperature: _____

Ingredients: Instructions:

Wine Pairing: _____

Notes:

Recipe:

Serving: _____   Prep Time: _____

Cook Time: _____   Temperature: _____

Ingredients: Instructions:

_____   _____
_____   _____
_____   _____
_____   _____
_____   _____
_____   _____
_____   _____
_____   _____
_____   _____
_____   _____
_____   _____
_____   _____
_____   _____
_____   _____

Wine Pairing: _____

Notes:

Recipe: _____

Serving: _____   Prep Time: _____

Cook Time: _____   Temperature: _____

Ingredients: Instructions:
_____   _____
_____   _____
_____   _____
_____   _____
_____   _____
_____   _____
_____   _____
_____   _____
_____   _____
_____   _____
_____   _____
_____   _____
_____   _____
_____   _____
_____   _____
_____   _____

Wine Pairing: _____

Notes: _____

Recipe:

Serving: Prep Time:

Cook Time: Temperature:

Ingredients: Instructions:

Wine Pairing:

Notes:

Recipe: _____

Serving: _____   Prep Time: _____

Cook Time: _____   Temperature: _____

Ingredients: Instructions:

_____   _____
_____   _____
_____   _____
_____   _____
_____   _____
_____   _____
_____   _____
_____   _____
_____   _____
_____   _____
_____   _____
_____   _____
_____   _____
_____   _____

Wine Pairing: _____

Notes: _____

Recipe: _____

Serving: _____   Prep Time: _____

Cook Time: _____   Temperature: _____

Ingredients: Instructions:

_____   _____
_____   _____
_____   _____
_____   _____
_____   _____
_____   _____
_____   _____
_____   _____
_____   _____
_____   _____
_____   _____
_____   _____
_____   _____
_____   _____
_____   _____
_____   _____
_____   _____

Wine Pairing: _____

Notes: _____

Recipe:

Serving: _____ Prep Time: _____

Cook Time: _____ Temperature: _____

Ingredients: Instructions:

Wine Pairing: _____

Notes: _____

Recipe:

Serving: _____   Prep Time: _____

Cook Time: _____   Temperature: _____

Ingredients: Instructions:

_____   _____
_____   _____
_____   _____
_____   _____
_____   _____
_____   _____
_____   _____
_____   _____
_____   _____
_____   _____
_____   _____
_____   _____
_____   _____
_____   _____
_____   _____
_____   _____

Wine Pairing: _____

Notes: _____

Recipe: _____

Serving: _____ Prep Time: _____

Cook Time: _____ Temperature: _____

Ingredients: Instructions:

_____ _____
_____ _____
_____ _____
_____ _____
_____ _____
_____ _____
_____ _____
_____ _____
_____ _____
_____ _____
_____ _____
_____ _____
_____ _____
_____ _____
_____ _____
_____ _____

Wine Pairing: _____

Notes: _____

Recipe: _____

Serving: _____   Prep Time: _____

Cook Time: _____   Temperature: _____

Ingredients: Instructions:

_____   _____
_____   _____
_____   _____
_____   _____
_____   _____
_____   _____
_____   _____
_____   _____
_____   _____
_____   _____
_____   _____
_____   _____
_____   _____
_____   _____
_____   _____
_____   _____
_____   _____
_____   _____

Wine Pairing: _____

Notes: _____

Recipe: _____

Serving: _____   Prep Time: _____

Cook Time: _____   Temperature: _____

Ingredients: Instructions:

_____   _____
_____   _____
_____   _____
_____   _____
_____   _____
_____   _____
_____   _____
_____   _____
_____   _____
_____   _____
_____   _____
_____   _____
_____   _____
_____   _____
_____   _____
_____   _____

Wine Pairing: _____

Notes: _____

Recipe: _____

Serving: _____ Prep Time: _____

Cook Time: _____ Temperature: _____

Ingredients:

_____

_____

_____

_____

_____

_____

_____

_____

_____

_____

_____

_____

_____

_____

_____

_____

_____

Instructions:

_____

_____

_____

_____

_____

_____

_____

_____

_____

_____

_____

_____

_____

_____

_____

_____

Wine Pairing: _____

Notes: _____

Recipe:

Serving: _____ Prep Time: _____

Cook Time: _____ Temperature: _____

Ingredients: Instructions:

Wine Pairing: _____

Notes:

Recipe: _____

Serving: _____   Prep Time: _____

Cook Time: _____   Temperature: _____

Ingredients: Instructions:

_____   _____
_____   _____
_____   _____
_____   _____
_____   _____
_____   _____
_____   _____
_____   _____
_____   _____
_____   _____
_____   _____
_____   _____
_____   _____
_____   _____
_____   _____

Wine Pairing: _____

Notes: _____

Recipe:

Serving: _____   Prep Time: _____

Cook Time: _____   Temperature: _____

Ingredients: Instructions:

Wine Pairing: _____

Notes:

Recipe: _____

Serving: _____   Prep Time: _____

Cook Time: _____   Temperature: _____

Ingredients: Instructions:

_____   _____
_____   _____
_____   _____
_____   _____
_____   _____
_____   _____
_____   _____
_____   _____
_____   _____
_____   _____
_____   _____
_____   _____
_____   _____
_____   _____
_____   _____
_____   _____
_____   _____
_____   _____

Wine Pairing: _____

Notes: _____

Recipe:

Serving: _____   Prep Time: _____

Cook Time: _____   Temperature: _____

Ingredients: Instructions:

Wine Pairing: _____

Notes: _____

Recipe:

Serving: _____   Prep Time: _____

Cook Time: _____   Temperature: _____

Ingredients: Instructions:

Wine Pairing: _____

Notes:

Recipe:

Serving: _____ Prep Time: _____

Cook Time: _____ Temperature: _____

Ingredients: Instructions:

Wine Pairing:

Notes:

Recipe:

Serving: _____ Prep Time: _____

Cook Time: _____ Temperature: _____

Ingredients: Instructions:

Wine Pairing: _____

Notes:

Recipe:

Serving: _____ Prep Time: _____

Cook Time: _____ Temperature: _____

Ingredients: Instructions:

Wine Pairing: _____

Notes:

Made in the USA
Monee, IL
06 March 2023

29255538R00090